EMBARK ON A JOURNEY OF PROFOUND CONVERSATION: 250 QUESTIONS TO SPARK DEEP CONNECTIONS

ARE YOU READY TO DELVE BEYOND THE SURFACE OF EVERYDAY EXCHANGES AND IGNITE TRULY MEANINGFUL CONVERSATIONS? THIS COLLECTION OF 250 THOUGHT-PROVOKING QUESTIONS IS DESIGNED TO STIMULATE YOUR CURIOSITY, CHALLENGE YOUR PERSPECTIVES, AND FOSTER GENUINE CONNECTIONS WITH OTHERS.

FORGET THE WEATHER OR
CURRENT EVENTS – THESE
CAREFULLY CRAFTED INQUIRIES
DELVE INTO THE DEPTHS OF HUMAN
EXPERIENCE. WE'LL EXPLORE THE
REALMS OF CREATIVITY,
VULNERABILITY, AMBITION, AND
EVERYTHING IN BETWEEN. IMAGINE
DISCUSSIONS THAT LINGER LONG
AFTER THE LAST WORD IS SPOKEN,
LEAVING YOU WITH A RENEWED
APPRECIATION FOR THE
COMPLEXITY AND WONDER OF
HUMAN THOUGHT.

THIS ISN'T JUST A LIST OF QUESTIONS; IT'S AN INVITATION TO EMBARK ON A CAPTIVATING JOURNEY OF SELF-DISCOVERY AND CONNECTION. PREPARE TO BE SURPRISED, CHALLENGED, AND DEEPLY MOVED AS YOU EXPLORE THE VAST LANDSCAPES OF HUMAN EXPERIENCE. SO, GATHER YOUR CLOSEST COMPANIONS, IGNITE YOUR CURIOSITY, AND LET THE CONVERSATIONS BEGIN!

1.   IF YOU COULD CREATE A NEW HUMAN SENSE, WHAT WOULD IT BE AND WHY?

2.   IMAGINE A WORLD WITHOUT TIMEKEEPING. HOW WOULD IT CHANGE OUR PERCEPTION OF LIFE?

3. IF YOU COULD CURATE A MUSEUM EXHIBIT ON YOUR OWN LIFE, WHAT ARTIFACTS WOULD YOU DISPLAY AND WHAT STORIES WOULD THEY TELL?

4. DO YOU BELIEVE IN THE CONCEPT OF A "SOULMATE"? WHY OR WHY NOT?

5. WHAT HISTORICAL EVENT RESONATES WITH YOU THE MOST ON A PERSONAL LEVEL?

6. IF YOU COULD TRAVEL BACK IN TIME AND OBSERVE ONE EVENT, WHAT WOULD IT BE AND WHY?

7. CAN YOU DESCRIBE A TURNING POINT IN YOUR LIFE THAT SHAPED WHO YOU ARE TODAY?

8. WHAT FICTIONAL UTOPIA FROM LITERATURE OR FILM SEEMS MOST APPEALING TO YOU, AND WHY?

9 .LET'S SAY YOU WIN THE LOTTERY BUT WITH A TWIST: THE MONEY COMES WITH A RANDOM QUIRK OR SOCIAL CAUSE YOU MUST CHAMPION. WHAT WOULD YOU PICK AND HOW WOULD YOU USE THE FUNDS?

10. IF YOU COULD SPEAK FLUENTLY IN THE LANGUAGE OF ANY ANIMAL, WHICH WOULD YOU CHOOSE AND WHAT WOULD YOU BE MOST CURIOUS TO LEARN FROM THEM?

11. DO YOU THINK ARTIFICIAL INTELLIGENCE WILL EVER TRULY UNDERSTAND HUMAN EMOTIONS?

12. WHAT UNSOLVED HISTORICAL MYSTERY FASCINATES YOU THE MOST?

13. IMAGINE YOU COULD BOTTLE
AND SELL A SPECIFIC EMOTION.
WHAT EMOTION WOULD IT BE AND
HOW WOULD YOU MARKET IT?

14. WHAT DOES THE CONCEPT OF
"BEAUTY" MEAN TO YOU, AND DO
YOU THINK IT'S UNIVERSAL OR
CULTURALLY DEFINED?

15. IF YOU COULD DESIGN A COURSE
TO BE MANDATORY IN EVERY
SCHOOL CURRICULUM, WHAT
SUBJECT WOULD YOU CHOOSE AND
WHY?

16. WHAT FICTIONAL CHARACTER
DO YOU FIND STRANGELY
RELATABLE, AND WHY?

17. HAVE YOU EVER HAD AN EXPERIENCE THAT CHALLENGED YOUR BELIEFS ABOUT THE SUPERNATURAL OR PARANORMAL?

18. WHAT PERSONAL FEAR DO YOU THINK WOULD BE MOST INTERESTING TO EXPLORE IN A FICTIONAL STORY?

19. LET'S SAY YOU COULD LIVE FOREVER, BUT YOU WOULD AGE VERY SLOWLY. WOULD YOU TAKE THE DEAL AND WHY OR WHY NOT?

20. WHAT HISTORICAL FIGURE DO YOU THINK IS MOST MISUNDERSTOOD, AND HOW WOULD YOU REFRAME THEIR STORY?

21. IF YOU COULD CREATE A HOLIDAY DEDICATED TO A SPECIFIC VALUE, WHAT WOULD IT BE AND HOW WOULD IT BE CELEBRATED?

22. WHAT CREATIVE PURSUIT DO YOU WISH YOU HAD MORE TIME TO EXPLORE?

23. WHAT DO YOU THINK HAPPENS AFTER WE DIE?

24. WHAT DOES TRUE LEADERSHIP LOOK LIKE TO YOU?

25. WHEN WAS THE LAST TIME YOU CHANGED YOUR MIND ABOUT SOMETHING SIGNIFICANT?

26. WHAT LIFE LESSON HAS BEEN THE MOST DIFFICULT FOR YOU TO LEARN?

27. DO YOU BELIEVE IN THE CONCEPT OF "GUT INSTINCT"?

28. WHAT BRINGS YOU THE MOST JOY IN YOUR EVERYDAY LIFE?

29. WHAT DOES FORGIVENESS
TRULY MEAN TO YOU?

30. WHAT LEGACY WOULD YOU LIKE
TO LEAVE BEHIND?

31. WHAT HISTORICAL PERIOD
WOULD YOU LOVE TO HAVE A
FRONT-ROW SEAT TO, AND WHY?

32. WHAT SOCIAL ISSUE ARE YOU
MOST PASSIONATE ABOUT AND
WHY?

33. IF YOU COULD HAVE ANY SUPERPOWER, WHAT WOULD IT BE AND HOW WOULD YOU USE IT?

34. WHAT DOES TRUE FRIENDSHIP MEAN TO YOU?

35. WHAT DOES INNER PEACE LOOK LIKE FOR YOU?

36. WHAT IS THE GREATEST INVENTION OF HUMANITY, IN YOUR OPINION?

37. WHAT SCIENTIFIC DISCOVERY
WOULD HAVE THE BIGGEST POSITIVE
IMPACT ON THE WORLD?

38. WHAT DOES THE CONCEPT OF
"HOME" MEAN TO YOU?

39. WHAT FICTIONAL WORLD
WOULD YOU LOVE TO INHABIT, AND
WHY?

40. WHAT DOES TRUE FREEDOM
LOOK LIKE TO YOU?

41. WHAT IS THE BRAVEST THING YOU'VE EVER DONE?

42. WHAT CREATIVE MEDIUM (PAINTING, MUSIC, WRITING, ETC.) DO YOU FIND MOST EXPRESSIVE, AND WHY?

43. WHAT HISTORICAL FIGURE DO YOU ADMIRE THE MOST, AND WHY?

44. WHAT DOES THE CONCEPT OF "RISK" MEAN TO YOU?

45. WHAT IS THE QUALITY YOU
ADMIRE MOST IN OTHERS?

46. WHAT IS THE MOST IMPORTANT
THING YOU'VE LEARNED FROM
FAILURE?

47. WHAT DOES THE CONCEPT OF
"SUCCESS" MEAN TO YOU?

48. WHAT IS THE BIGGEST
CHALLENGE FACING HUMANITY
TODAY?

49. WHAT ETHICAL DILEMMA HAVE YOU GRAPPLED WITH THE MOST?

50. WHAT DOES TRUE HAPPINESS LOOK LIKE TO YOU?

51. IMAGINE YOU COULD HAVE A CONVERSATION WITH YOUR YOUNGER SELF. WHAT ADVICE WOULD YOU GIVE THEM?

52. WHAT DOES THE CONCEPT OF "PURPOSE" MEAN TO YOU?

53. WHAT FICTIONAL VILLAIN DO YOU FIND STRANGELY SYMPATHETIC, AND WHY?

54. WHAT CURRENT TREND DO YOU THINK WILL HAVE THE MOST LASTING IMPACT ON SOCIETY?

55. WHAT MAKES A GOOD APOLOGY, IN YOUR OPINION?

56. WHAT DOES TRUE COURAGE LOOK LIKE TO YOU?

57. WHAT DOES TRUE COURAGE LOOK LIKE TO YOU?

58. WHAT IS THE MOST BEAUTIFUL NATURAL PLACE YOU'VE EVER VISITED?

59. WHAT DOES THE CONCEPT OF "TRUTH" MEAN TO YOU IN A WORLD OF MISINFORMATION?

60. WHAT IS THE QUESTION YOU'RE MOST AFRAID TO ASK?
WHAT DOES THE CONCEPT OF "CIVILIZATION" MEAN TO YOU?

61. WHAT HISTORICAL ARTIFACT WOULD YOU LOVE TO SEE IN PERSON, AND WHY?

62. WHAT DOES THE CONCEPT OF "LUCK" MEAN TO YOU?

63. WHAT FICTIONAL LOVE STORY RESONATES WITH YOU THE MOST, AND WHY?

64. WHAT IS THE WEIRDEST DREAM YOU'VE EVER HAD, AND HOW DID IT AFFECT YOU?

65. WHAT DOES THE CONCEPT OF "GRATITUDE" MEAN TO YOU?

66. WHAT IS THE BEST PIECE OF ADVICE YOU'VE EVER RECEIVED?

67. WHAT DOES THE CONCEPT OF "FORGIVENESS" MEAN TO YOU?

68. WHAT FICTIONAL COMING-OF-AGE STORY RESONATES WITH YOU THE MOST, AND WHY?

69. WHAT IS THE MOST IMPORTANT THING YOU'VE LEARNED ABOUT YOURSELF IN THE PAST YEAR?

70. WHAT CREATIVE SKILL DO YOU WISH YOU WERE BETTER AT?

71. WHAT HISTORICAL FIGURE DO YOU THINK IS MOST UNDERRATED, AND WHY?

72. WHAT DOES THE CONCEPT OF "AMBITION" MEAN TO YOU?

73. WHAT IS THE QUALITY YOU VALUE MOST IN YOURSELF?

74. WHAT DOES THE CONCEPT OF "BALANCE" MEAN TO YOU IN A BUSY WORLD?

75. WHAT FICTIONAL TEACHER OR MENTOR DO YOU FIND MOST INSPIRING, AND WHY?

76. WHAT IS THE BRAVEST THING YOU'VE EVER WITNESSED SOMEONE ELSE DO?

77. WHAT ARTISTIC MOVEMENT
(RENAISSANCE, IMPRESSIONISM, ETC.)
RESONATES WITH YOU THE MOST,
AND WHY?

78. WHAT HISTORICAL PERIOD ARE
YOU MOST CURIOUS TO LEARN
MORE ABOUT?

79. WHAT SOCIAL CAUSE ARE YOU
WILLING TO FIGHT FOR?

80. WHAT DOES THE CONCEPT OF
"SACRIFICE" MEAN TO YOU?

81. IF YOU COULD TRAVEL ANYWHERE IN SPACE, WHERE WOULD YOU GO AND WHY?

82. WHAT FICTIONAL WORLD DO YOU THINK WOULD BE THE MOST DANGEROUS TO INHABIT, AND WHY?

83. WHAT CURRENT EVENT DO YOU THINK WILL BE A MAJOR TURNING POINT IN HISTORY?

84. WHAT MAKES A GOOD CONVERSATION, IN YOUR OPINION?

85. WHAT DOES THE CONCEPT OF "CREATIVITY" MEAN TO YOU?

86. WHAT IS THE BRAVEST THING YOU'VE EVER DONE TO STAND UP FOR WHAT YOU BELIEVE IN?

87. WHAT NATURAL WONDER LEAVES YOU MOST AWESTRUCK?

88. WHAT DOES THE CONCEPT OF "CURIOSITY" MEAN TO YOU?

89. WHAT FICTIONAL DETECTIVE OR INVESTIGATOR DO YOU FIND MOST ADMIRABLE, AND WHY?

90. WHAT IS THE WEIRDEST OR MOST INTERESTING CONSPIRACY THEORY YOU'VE HEARD?

91. WHAT DOES THE CONCEPT OF "PROGRESS" MEAN TO YOU?

92. WHAT HISTORICAL FIGURE DO YOU THINK IS MOST OVERRATED, AND WHY?

93. WHAT IS THE BIGGEST RISK YOU'RE WILLING TO TAKE IN YOUR LIFE?

94. WHAT QUALITY DO YOU FIND MOST ATTRACTIVE IN A PERSON (BEYOND PHYSICAL APPEARANCE)?

95. WHAT DOES THE CONCEPT OF "PASSION" MEAN TO YOU?

96. WHAT FICTIONAL VILLAIN DO YOU FIND MOST TERRIFYING, AND WHY?

97. WHAT CURRENT SOCIAL ISSUE ARE YOU MOST OPTIMISTIC ABOUT OVERCOMING?

98. WHAT DOES THE CONCEPT OF "HOPE" MEAN TO YOU?

99. WHAT IS THE MOST IMPORTANT THING YOU WANT TO LEARN IN THE NEXT YEAR?

100. WHAT CREATIVE HOBBY DO YOU WISH YOU HAD MORE TIME FOR?

101. IMAGINE YOU COULD HOLD A GLOBAL CONFERENCE ON ANY TOPIC. WHAT WOULD IT BE ABOUT AND WHAT MESSAGE WOULD YOU WANT TO CONVEY?

102. WHAT FICTIONAL HERO DO YOU FIND MOST INSPIRING, AND WHY?

103. WHAT IS THE BRAVEST THING YOU'VE OVERCOME IN YOUR LIFE?

104. WHAT ARTISTIC MEDIUM (PAINTING, MUSIC, WRITING, ETC.) DO YOU FIND MOST CHALLENGING, AND WHY?

105. WHAT HISTORICAL EVENT DO YOU THINK IS MOST UNDER-REPORTED?

106. WHAT SOCIAL CAUSE ARE YOU ACTIVELY INVOLVED IN?

107. IF YOU COULD HAVE A SUPERPOWER THAT ONLY WORKED BEHIND THE SCENES, ANONYMOUSLY HELPING PEOPLE, WOULD YOU TAKE IT? WHY OR WHY NOT?

108. WHAT DOES THE CONCEPT OF "JUSTICE" MEAN TO YOU IN A COMPLEX WORLD?

109. WHAT IS THE BIGGEST CHALLENGE YOU'RE FACING RIGHT NOW?

110. WHAT FICTIONAL FRIENDSHIP DO YOU FIND MOST HEARTWARMING, AND WHY?

111. WHAT HISTORICAL FIGURE WOULD YOU LOVE TO DEBATE A CURRENT ISSUE WITH, AND WHY?

112. WHAT DOES THE CONCEPT OF "COMPASSION" MEAN TO YOU?

113. WHAT FICTIONAL CREATURE DO YOU FIND MOST FASCINATING, AND WHY?

114. WHAT CURRENT INVENTION DO YOU THINK IS MOST UNDERRATED?

115. WHAT DOES THE CONCEPT OF "EMPATHY" MEAN TO YOU?

116.WHAT IS THE BRAVEST ACT OF KINDNESS YOU'VE EVER WITNESSED?

117. WHAT MUSICAL GENRE DO YOU FIND MOST EMOTIONALLY RESONANT, AND WHY?

118. WHAT DOES THE CONCEPT OF "IMAGINATION" MEAN TO YOU?

119. WHAT FICTIONAL PROPHECY DO YOU FIND MOST BELIEVABLE, AND WHY?

120. WHAT IS THE WEIRDEST OR MOST INTERESTING DREAM YOU'VE HAD RECENTLY, AND HOW DID IT AFFECT YOU?

121. IF YOU COULD CURATE A MUSEUM EXHIBIT ON A SPECIFIC EMOTION, WHICH EMOTION WOULD YOU CHOOSE AND HOW WOULD YOU SHOWCASE IT?

122. WHAT FICTIONAL FAMILY DYNAMIC RESONATES WITH YOU THE MOST, AND WHY?

123. WHAT IS THE BRAVEST THING YOU'VE DONE FOR LOVE?

124. WHAT LITERARY GENRE DO YOU FIND MOST INTELLECTUALLY STIMULATING, AND WHY?

125. WHAT HISTORICAL FIGURE DO YOU THINK HISTORY HAS BEEN MOST CRUEL TO?

126. WHAT SOCIAL CAUSE ARE YOU SECRETLY PASSIONATE ABOUT BUT HAVEN'T SPOKEN UP FOR YET?

127. IMAGINE YOU COULD TIME TRAVEL, BUT YOU COULD ONLY GO A FEW HOURS INTO THE FUTURE. WOULD YOU USE IT AND WHY OR WHY NOT?

128. WHAT DOES THE CONCEPT OF "MORALITY" MEAN TO YOU IN A WORLD OF DIVERSE CULTURES?

129. WHAT IS THE BIGGEST MISCONCEPTION ABOUT YOU?

130. WHAT FICTIONAL VILLAIN DO YOU FIND MOST UNDERSTANDABLE, AND WHY?

131. WHAT CURRENT EVENT DO YOU THINK IS GETTING THE MOST SENSATIONALIZED COVERAGE?

132. WHAT DOES THE CONCEPT OF "COMMUNICATION" MEAN TO YOU IN A WORLD OF SOCIAL MEDIA?

133. WHAT FICTIONAL ANTI-HERO DO YOU FIND MOST COMPELLING, AND WHY?

134. WHAT UNSOLVED MYSTERY IN YOUR OWN LIFE ARE YOU MOST CURIOUS TO UNRAVEL?

135. WHAT DOES THE CONCEPT OF "IDENTITY" MEAN TO YOU IN A CONSTANTLY CHANGING WORLD?

136. WHAT IS THE BRAVEST THING YOU'VE DONE TO STAND UP FOR YOURSELF?

137. WHAT ARTISTIC DISCIPLINE (PAINTING, MUSIC, DANCE, ETC.) DO YOU FIND MOST MOVING, AND WHY?

138. WHAT DOES THE CONCEPT OF "CURIOSITY" MEAN TO YOU AS AN ADULT?

139. WHAT FICTIONAL COMING-OF-AGE STORY DO YOU THINK IS MOST RELEVANT TODAY, AND WHY?

140. WHAT IS THE MOST IMPORTANT SKILL YOU'VE LEARNED IN THE PAST YEAR?

141. WHAT FICTIONAL WORLD DO YOU THINK WOULD BE THE MOST BORING TO INHABIT, AND WHY?

142. WHAT CURRENT TREND DO YOU THINK IS MOST HARMFUL TO SOCIETY?

143. WHAT MAKES A GOOD APOLOGY, IN YOUR OPINION?

144. WHAT DOES THE CONCEPT OF "RESILIENCE" MEAN TO YOU?

145. WHAT IS THE BRAVEST THING YOU'VE WITNESSED SOMEONE ELSE OVERCOME?

146. WHAT ARTISTIC MOVEMENT (RENAISSANCE, POP ART, ETC.) DO YOU FIND MOST OVERRATED, AND WHY?

147. WHAT HISTORICAL PERIOD ARE YOU MOST GLAD YOU DON'T LIVE IN, AND WHY?

148. WHAT SOCIAL CAUSE ARE YOU SURPRISED DOESN'T GET MORE ATTENTION?

149. WHAT DOES THE CONCEPT OF "RESPONSIBILITY" MEAN TO YOU?

150. WHAT FICTIONAL SACRIFICE RESONATES WITH YOU THE MOST, AND WHY?

151. IMAGINE YOU COULD DESIGN A SOCIAL MEDIA PLATFORM WITH A SPECIFIC FOCUS. WHAT WOULD IT BE DESIGNED TO ENCOURAGE?

152. WHAT FICTIONAL HERO DO YOU FIND MOST RELATABLE, AND WHY?

153. WHAT IS THE BIGGEST CHALLENGE YOU'VE OVERCOME IN YOUR RELATIONSHIPS?

154. WHAT LITERARY GENRE DO YOU FIND MOST COMFORTING, AND WHY?

155. WHAT HISTORICAL FIGURE DO YOU THINKWOULD BE THE MOST SURPRISED BY THE WAY THE WORLD HAS CHANGED?

156. WHAT SOCIAL CAUSE DO YOU THINK FUTURE GENERATIONS WILL LOOK BACK ON AND WONDER WHY WE DIDN'T ADDRESS IT SOONER?

157. IF YOU COULD CREATE A NEW RIGHT TO BE ENSHRINED IN LAW, WHAT WOULD IT BE?

158. WHAT DOES THE CONCEPT OF "FREEDOM OF SPEECH" MEAN TO YOU IN THE AGE OF ONLINE ANONYMITY?

159. WHAT IS THE BRAVEST ACT OF SELFLESSNESS YOU'VE EVER WITNESSED?

160. WHAT ARTISTIC MEDIUM (PAINTING, MUSIC, WRITING, ETC.) DO YOU FIND MOST DIFFICULT TO UNDERSTAND, AND WHY?

161. WHAT UNSOLVED QUESTION ABOUT THE NATURAL WORLD FASCINATES YOU THE MOST?

162. WHAT FICTIONAL BETRAYAL DO YOU FIND MOST SHOCKING, AND WHY?

163. WHAT IS THE BRAVEST THING YOU'VE DONE TO STEP OUTSIDE YOUR COMFORT ZONE?

164. WHAT ARTISTIC DISCIPLINE (PAINTING, MUSIC, DANCE, ETC.) DO YOU FIND MOST INTIMIDATING, AND WHY?

165. WHAT DOES THE CONCEPT OF "WONDER" MEAN TO YOU AS AN ADULT?

166. WHAT FICTIONAL UTOPIA SEEMS MOST UNREALISTIC, AND WHY?

167. WHAT CURRENT SCIENTIFIC DISCOVERY ARE YOU MOST EXCITED ABOUT?

168. WHAT DOES THE CONCEPT OF "GRATITUDE" LOOK LIKE IN PRACTICE FOR YOU?

169. WHAT FICTIONAL ACT OF REVENGE DO YOU FIND MOST SATISFYING, AND WHY?

170. IMAGINE YOU COULD CREATE A HOLIDAY DEDICATED TO A SPECIFIC SENSE. WHICH SENSE WOULD YOU CHOOSE AND HOW WOULD IT BE CELEBRATED?

171. WHAT FICTIONAL VILLAIN DO YOU FIND MOST PITIABLE, AND WHY?

172. WHAT CURRENT EVENT DO YOU THINK WILL HAVE THE MOST FAR-REACHING CONSEQUENCES?

173. WHAT MAKES A GOOD
LISTENER, IN YOUR OPINION?

174. WHAT DOES THE CONCEPT OF
"VULNERABILITY" MEAN TO YOU?

175. WHAT IS THE BRAVEST THING
YOU'VE DONE TO EXPRESS
YOURSELF AUTHENTICALLY?

176. WHAT ARTISTIC MOVEMENT
(RENAISSANCE, SURREALISM, ETC.)
DO YOU FIND MOST INSPIRING, AND
WHY?

177. WHAT HISTORICAL PERIOD ARE YOU MOST FASCINATED BY, AND WHY?

178. WHAT SOCIAL CAUSE DO YOU THINK NEEDS A COMPLETE REFRAMING OF THE CONVERSATION?

179. WHAT DOES THE CONCEPT OF "ACCOUNTABILITY" MEAN TO YOU?

180. IF YOU COULD CREATE A COURSE TO BE MANDATORY FOR EVERY ADULT, WHAT SUBJECT WOULD YOU CHOOSE AND WHY?

181. WHAT FICTIONAL CREATURE DO YOU FIND MOST TERRIFYING, AND WHY?

182. WHAT CURRENT INVENTION DO YOU THINK IS MOST OVERRATED?

183. WHAT DOES THE CONCEPT OF "EMPATHY" LOOK LIKE IN ACTION FOR YOU?

184. WHAT IS THE BRAVEST THING YOU'VE DONE TO CHALLENGE YOUR OWN ASSUMPTIONS?

185. WHAT ARTISTIC DISCIPLINE (PAINTING, MUSIC, DANCE, ETC.) DO YOU FIND MOST EXPRESSIVE FOR SOCIAL COMMENTARY?

186. WHAT DOES THE CONCEPT OF "CREATIVITY" MEAN TO YOU IN A WORLD SATURATED WITH INFORMATION?

187. WHAT FICTIONAL PROPHECY DO YOU FIND MOST DISTURBING, AND WHY?

188. WHAT IS THE MOST CHALLENGING ASPECT OF BEING HUMAN, IN YOUR OPINION?

189. WHAT FICTIONAL WORLD DO YOU THINK WOULD BE THE MOST DIFFICULT TO LEAVE BEHIND?

190. IMAGINE YOU COULD HOLD A GLOBAL CONFERENCE ON A SPECIFIC CHALLENGE FACING HUMANITY. WHAT WOULD IT BE AND WHAT SOLUTIONS WOULD YOU PROPOSE?

191. WHAT DOES THE CONCEPT OF "HOPE" LOOK LIKE IN THE FACE OF DESPAIR?

192. WHAT UNSOLVED MYSTERY IN HISTORY KEEPS YOU UP AT NIGHT?

193. WHAT LITERARY GENRE DO YOU FIND MOST CHALLENGING TO WRITE IN, AND WHY?

194. WHAT HISTORICAL FIGURE DO YOU THINK HAS THE MOST RELEVANT MESSAGE FOR OUR TIMES?

195. WHAT SOCIAL CAUSE ARE YOU ACTIVELY WORKING TOWARDS IN YOUR COMMUNITY?

196. IF YOU COULD HAVE A SUPERPOWER THAT CAME WITH A MAJOR DRAWBACK, WOULD YOU TAKE IT? WHY OR WHY NOT?

197. WHAT DOES THE CONCEPT OF "TRUTH" MEAN TO YOU IN A WORLD OF DIFFERING PERSPECTIVES?

198. WHAT IS THE BIGGEST MISCONCEPTION ABOUT YOUR GENERATION?

199. IMAGINE YOU COULD CURATE A MUSEUM EXHIBIT ON A SOUND. WHAT SOUND WOULD YOU CHOOSE AND HOW WOULD YOU USE IT TO TELL A STORY?

200. IF YOU COULD HAVE A MEANINGFUL CONVERSATION WITH A HISTORICAL FIGURE FROM ANY TIME PERIOD, WHO WOULD IT BE AND WHY?

201. WHAT FICTIONAL CHARACTER DO YOU THINK WOULD BE THE MOST INTERESTING DINNER GUEST, AND WHAT TOPICS WOULD YOU DISCUSS?

202. WHAT DOES THE CONCEPT OF "BEAUTY" MEAN TO YOU IN THE NATURAL WORLD?

203. WHAT UNSOLVED QUESTION ABOUT THE HUMAN MIND FASCINATES YOU THE MOST?

204. DO YOU BELIEVE IN THE CONCEPT OF "SOULMATES"? WHY OR WHY NOT, AND HOW WOULD YOU DEFINE ONE?

205. WHAT HISTORICAL EVENT DO YOU THINK HAS BEEN THE MOST ROMANTICIZED, AND WHY?

206. LET'S SAY YOU WIN THE LOTTERY BUT WITH A TWIST: THE MONEY COMES WITH A RANDOM ARTISTIC MEDIUM YOU MUST USE TO CREATE SOMETHING MEANINGFUL. WHAT WOULD YOU PICK AND WHAT WOULD YOU CREATE?

207. IF YOU COULD TRAVEL FREELY THROUGHOUT TIME, WOULD YOU CHOOSE TO VISIT THE PAST OR THE FUTURE, AND WHY?

208. WHAT FICTIONAL WORLD DO YOU THINK WOULD BE THE MOST DIFFICULT TO LEARN THE SOCIAL ETIQUETTE OF, AND WHY?

209. WHAT CURRENT SOCIAL ISSUE DO YOU THINK FUTURE GENERATIONS WILL BE MOST JUDGMENTAL ABOUT IN HINDSIGHT?

210. WHAT DOES THE CONCEPT OF "HAPPINESS" MEAN TO YOU IN A WORLD THAT CONSTANTLY BOMBARDS US WITH MESSAGES OF WHAT WE LACK?

211. WHAT HAS BEEN YOUR PROUDEST MOMENT OF GROWTH OR SELF-DISCOVERY?

212. WHAT FICTIONAL DETECTIVE WOULD YOU TRUST MOST TO SOLVE A REAL-LIFE MYSTERY, AND WHY?

213. WHAT DOES THE CONCEPT OF "RISK" LOOK DIFFERENT FOR IN DIFFERENT STAGES OF LIFE?

214. WHAT HISTORICAL FIGURE DO YOU THINK IS MOST MISUNDERSTOOD BY THE GENERAL PUBLIC?

215. WHAT CURRENT INVENTION DO YOU THINK HAS THE MOST POTENTIAL TO NEGATIVELY IMPACT SOCIETY IN THE LONG RUN?

216. WHAT DOES THE CONCEPT OF "LOVE" MEAN TO YOU IN ITS VARIOUS FORMS (ROMANTIC, PLATONIC, FAMILIAL)?

217. WHAT FICTIONAL VILLAIN DO YOU FIND MOST TRAGICALLY FLAWED, AND WHY?

218. WHAT CURRENT SOCIAL CAUSE DO YOU THINK IS MOST EFFECTIVELY ADDRESSED THROUGH HUMOR OR SATIRE?

219. IF YOU COULD DESIGN A VIDEO GAME THAT TACKLED A COMPLEX SOCIAL ISSUE, WHAT WOULD IT BE AND HOW WOULD IT PLAY?

220. WHAT DOES THE CONCEPT OF "HOME" MEAN TO YOU BEYOND JUST A PHYSICAL LOCATION?

221. WHAT HAS BEEN THE MOST UNEXPECTED SOURCE OF INSPIRATION IN YOUR LIFE?

222. WHAT ARTISTIC DISCIPLINE (PAINTING, MUSIC, DANCE, ETC.) DO YOU FIND MOST CATHARTIC, AND WHY?

223. WHAT DOES THE CONCEPT OF "TIME" MEAN TO YOU, ESPECIALLY IN A WORLD THAT FEELS INCREASINGLY FAST-PACED?

224. WHAT HISTORICAL FIGURE DO YOU THINK WOULD BE THE MOST SURPRISED BY THE TECHNOLOGICAL ADVANCEMENTS OF TODAY?

225. WHAT CURRENT TREND DO YOU THINK IS MOST LIKELY TO BE A FAD AND FADE AWAY IN THE COMING YEARS?

226. WHAT DOES THE CONCEPT OF "CURIOSITY" LOOK LIKE IN ADULTHOOD, AND HOW DO YOU KEEP YOURS ALIVE?

227. WHAT FICTIONAL COMING-OF-AGE STORY DO YOU THINK RESONATES MOST WITH THE CHALLENGES YOUNG PEOPLE FACE TODAY?

228. WHAT IS THE MOST IMPORTANT SKILL YOU'VE LEARNED THROUGH TRIAL AND ERROR?

229. WHAT FICTIONAL WORLD DO YOU THINK WOULD BE THE MOST ETHICALLY COMPLEX TO LIVE IN, AND WHY?

230. WHAT CURRENT EVENT DO YOU THINK IS GETTING THE LEAST AMOUNT OF ATTENTION IT DESERVES?

231. WHAT MAKES A GOOD APOLOGY, IN YOUR OPINION?

232. WHAT DOES THE CONCEPT OF "RESILIENCE" MEAN TO YOU, AND HOW DO YOU CULTIVATE IT IN YOURSELF?

233. WHAT IS THE BRAVEST THING YOU'VE WITNESSED SOMEONE ELSE OVERCOME IN THE FACE OF ADVERSITY?

234. WHAT ARTISTIC MOVEMENT (RENAISSANCE, POP ART, ETC.) DO YOU FIND MOST UNDERRATED, AND WHY?

235. WHAT HISTORICAL PERIOD DO YOU THINK WOULD BE THE MOST CHALLENGING TO ADAPT TO CULTURALLY, AND WHY?

236. WHAT SOCIAL CAUSE ARE YOU SURPRISED DOESN'T GET MORE ATTENTION CONSIDERING ITS IMPACT?

237. WHAT DOES THE CONCEPT OF "RESPONSIBILITY" MEAN TO YOU ON A PERSONAL AND GLOBAL LEVEL?

238. WHAT FICTIONAL SACRIFICE DO YOU FIND MOST INSPIRING, AND WHY?

239. IMAGINE YOU COULD CREATE A SOCIAL MEDIA PLATFORM WITH A FOCUS ON A SPECIFIC HUMAN VALUE.
240. WHICH VALUE WOULD YOU CHOOSE AND HOW WOULD THE PLATFORM BE DESIGNED TO ENCOURAGE THAT VALUE?

241. WHAT FICTIONAL CREATURE DO YOU FIND MOST MISUNDERSTOOD, AND WHY?

242. WHAT CURRENT SCIENTIFIC DISCOVERY ARE YOU MOST OPTIMISTIC ABOUT FOR THE FUTURE OF HUMANITY?

243. WHAT DOES THE CONCEPT OF "GRATITUDE" LOOK LIKE IN ACTION IN YOUR DAILY LIFE?

244. WHAT FICTIONAL BETRAYAL DO YOU FIND MOST HEARTBREAKING, AND WHY?

245. WHAT IS THE BRAVEST THING YOU'VE DONE TO STAND UP FOR WHAT YOU BELIEVE IN, EVEN WHEN IT WASN'T POPULAR?

246. WHAT ARTISTIC MEDIUM (PAINTING, MUSIC, WRITING, ETC.) DO YOU FIND MOST EFFECTIVE FOR SOCIAL COMMENTARY, AND WHY?

247. WHAT DOES THE CONCEPT OF "LEGACY" MEAN TO YOU? HOW DO YOU WANT TO BE REMEMBERED?

248. WHAT FICTIONAL WORLD DO YOU THINK WOULD BE THE MOST LIBERATING TO LIVE IN, AND WHY?

249. IMAGINE YOU HAVE ALL THE MONEY IN THE WORLD, WHAT WOULD YOU DO WITH IT?

250. WHAT DOES THE CONCEPT OF "TRUTH" MEAN TO YOU IN A WORLD WHERE INFORMATION IS CONSTANTLY BEING FILTERED AND MANIPULATED?

THE ECHOING END: A CALL TO CONTINUED CONVERSATION

AS YOU REACH THE FINAL QUESTION OF THIS COLLECTION, A QUIET HUM OF POSSIBILITY MIGHT LINGER. THE CONVERSATIONS SPARKED MAY HAVE LEFT YOU EXHILARATED, INTROSPECTIVE, OR PERHAPS A TOUCH BEWILDERED. THAT'S THE BEAUTY OF DEEP DIALOGUE — IT DOESN'T ALWAYS PROVIDE ANSWERS, BUT IT IGNITES A FLAME OF CURIOSITY THAT CAN ILLUMINATE NEW PATHWAYS WITHIN OURSELVES AND OUR RELATIONSHIPS.

REMEMBER, THESE QUESTIONS ARE NOT MERE CONVERSATION STARTERS; THEY ARE SEEDS WAITING TO BE PLANTED IN FERTILE GROUND. ALLOW THEM TO TAKE ROOT IN YOUR MIND, AND WATCH AS THEY BLOSSOM INTO DEEPER CONNECTIONS, BOLDER SELF-DISCOVERY, AND A RENEWED APPRECIATION FOR THE RICHNESS OF HUMAN INTERACTION.

DON'T BE AFRAID TO REVISIT THESE INQUIRIES. AS YOUR EXPERIENCES AND PERSPECTIVES EVOLVE, SO TOO WILL THE ANSWERS YOU FIND WITHIN YOURSELF. SHARE THESE QUESTIONS WITH FRIENDS, FAMILY, AND EVEN STRANGERS. LET THEM BE A CATALYST FOR FORGING NEW BONDS AND FOSTERING DEEPER UNDERSTANDINGS.

THE WORLD IS A TAPESTRY WOVEN FROM COUNTLESS CONVERSATIONS, EACH THREAD ADDING ITS UNIQUE COLOR AND TEXTURE. BY ENGAGING IN THOUGHTFUL DIALOGUE, WE CONTRIBUTE THREADS OF VULNERABILITY, HONESTY, AND INTELLECTUAL CURIOSITY. LET THIS COLLECTION BE YOUR LOOM, AND LET YOUR CONVERSATIONS BE THE VIBRANT TAPESTRY YOU WEAVE.

SO GO FORTH, ARMED WITH THESE QUESTIONS AND AN OPEN HEART. EMBRACE THE POWER OF MEANINGFUL DIALOGUE. REMEMBER, THE MOST PROFOUND CONVERSATIONS OFTEN BEGIN WITH A SINGLE, WELL-CHOSEN QUESTION. LET YOURS BEGIN NOW.

REMEMBER

ALWAYS

BE KIND

TO YOURSELF

AND OTHERS

THANKS